CONSCIOUS TOGETHERNESS
A Love-affair

Zsa Zsa Tudos

AKIA Publishing

Second Edition

Published by AKIA Publishing

Copyright © *Zsa Zsa Tudos 2021*

https://zsazsatudos.com

For those who tipped the scale, and as an encouragement for those who hesitate to step on the path of man's greatest love affair, the one with LIFE.

Content

Foreword   6

The soul's journey   11

The contracts   32

The spirit guides   39

The family   51

The code   67

The thoughts   76

The relationships   91

The emotions   101

The insecurity   110

The empathy   120

The anxiety   128

The depression   133

The decision making   140

The conscious togetherness   146

The therapy   166

AKIA Philosophy   168

"By learning, you remember your knowledge;

With practice it becomes experience;

By teaching, you remind others of their knowledge."

FOREWORD

My thirty years of publishing, educating and coaching experience convinced me that the vast majority of earthlings do not understand life. It comes from the fact that the beginning of the journey is covered with all kinds of mysterious layers. The biggest mistake of earthlings is to focus on the end of the road, the aim, short of proper comprehension of the starting point.

Without beginning there is no road, only hovering and floating in a self-appointed bubble that brings false justification for existence.

Having said that, the beginning is the hardest to clarify, for humanity puts gap-filling layers on everything it touches, most of which stay there and by time, amalgamate into the core and used instantaneously as valid points in history, spirituality and knowledge. This action usually overrides all possible arguments or clarifications that emerge at a later stage.

However, all these layers take at least one valid point from the core. I created AKIA Philosophy to free these cores and build a matrix of interrelated energies and events, without succumbing to glorifying or comfort-building illusions and liberating the mind in the process.

The downfall is from the point of view. Earthlings started to alter their approach to everything during the Pisces era. Cut things up to pieces and eventually destroyed the essence. It is the same with human behaviour or any so-called scientific facts.

In ancient times scientists and philosophers looked at the global picture. Since they understood the interrelations of energies and the fact that the present shapes the future, there was never the question of polluting the air or eliminating the rainforests. It was the time when earthlings still comprehended the real and only important laws of attraction without focusing on personal gains and overriding the future of their children.

However, it is very difficult to say it out loud for people just bite your head off and throw it to the pigs. They do it without consideration or second thought. They don't have one. Only one option exists. The one they understand. So how can one learn? Talking about abuse, empathy and anxiety, the bookshelves are full of best sellers who are nurturing the ill feelings without offering a tangible way out.

I cannot emphasise it strongly enough that any kind of change in the behaviour pattern or belief system is hard work. And this work starts with the willingness of the people involved. Educators, in the real sense, are usually do not become famous or beloved in their time, for earthlings do not like changes. And the great irony is that they do not like to use their brain, the only thing that makes them different from every living creature on the planet.

In this book, I talk about the missing factors that make our lives misunderstood, fearful and miserable, adding the real intent of spreading essential keywords and lending sufficient courage to the reader to initiate the changes needed.

And since I plan to stay on the planet for a bit longer, you know where to find me in case of valid questions forming in your brain.

Have fun!

"Time is an illusion that imprisons those without courage"

AKIA-PATH-FINDER 1

THE SOUL'S JOURNEY

When somebody gives birth, in Spain they say *dar a luz*, meaning *give to light*. By doing it, one opens the possibility for an organic energy to grow. If this organic energy is guided and developed in the right way, it eventually becomes the source of light itself. It would reach the highest level of existence, the Sun man, the Ra that radiates and shines upon everything and everybody around, to ease the path. Therefore when a mother gives birth, she *gives light* and contributes to the possibility for a better existence.

In the Uranus era that had been lurking around since the 1950s, and came into full power in 2003, humanity talks about the various aspects of light with ease. However, they rarely mean the above-mentioned Spanish verb. There are Light-workers, Light-eaters, Warriors of Light, Light-beings, Light-healers and I could go on and on and on.

Light-workers are earthlings who understand the energies of the universe. They are healers of the planet. The Warriors of Light are earthlings who fight for the Light. Light-eaters can digest light and do not need food. However, it only is an illusion, for physical existence needs food. Light-beings are those, who incarnate onto Earth from time to time carrying important tasks. Light-healers heal with light. And Light givers invite souls down to Earth to fit into the ready-made costume generally called the physical body and become an earthling. However, this deed is usually subconscious and circles around gap-filling stories to provide a more favourable background.

Every organic life form on Earth needs light. When you put a seed into a pot of soil you usually hide it in the dark so it becomes stronger in this dormant state. Then it will be eager to get out of the dark and search for the life force of light. However, if the seed stays hidden for longer than supposed to, depression sets in and it might give up on life forever. When the shoot appears, the seed arrives at the next stage of its life and becomes a plant. This example stands for all organic energies including human beings.

In the very moment, the foetus is introduced to light and the umbilical cord is cut, an independent new life starts. It surely needs some nurturing, especially in the beginning, however, the aim is to make it strong and able for a successful earthly living while keeping the gate between the planet and the universe wide open. Religions are not fit to perform the task. Instead of fear, knowledge should be introduced and thinking encouraged. The ever-expanding universe follows the laws of physics and earthlings are part of this magic. They should feel at home in it by stretching their comfort zone into the universe.

Organic energies are living substances. I call them organic, for they use nature's gifts to maintain and improve themselves. They receive the necessary energy intake from other organic energies, such as vegetation and animal kingdom, for their physical survival. In addition, due to their connection with the macrocosm, human beings are influenced greatly by outside forces, like planets, the Solar System, the Galaxy and the whole matrix of the universe.

Souls from many planets are waiting for the opportunity to taste earthly living. Most of these planets, like Mars, Venus and Neptune, are in the same Solar System as Earth. Others, like Leo, Aries, Gemini or Cancer are part of the 12-star formations zodiac that *ruled* people for about 5 thousand years. Although they are not in alignment with the planet any longer, therefore their effect on Earth is almost non-existent, souls living there still favour Earth as an exciting destination to camp out for a while. The 22-star formations *Lost Zodiac* also willingly *lends* souls to be part of the miracle of the Birth of Light. Bearing all of this in mind Earth is like a school with only intensive courses that souls should enrol at least once in their infinite lifetime. The courses do not need entry exams and they all promise the opportunity of the necessary evolving as the sole purpose of all souls. When a soul decides to descend, it enrols in an *individual course* based upon its ability, strength, curiosity, courage and ambitions.

After making a decision, the soul comes into the Higher Plane of Earth, the upper layer of the planet's aura called Shambala, to discuss the possibilities. Here the soul meets the first set of guides who help tackle the initial years on Earth. There would be also somebody representing the Alpha & Omega Council of the universe to give an additional task to fulfil, and to help choose the family to be born into.

I am certain this description looks similar to a sci-fi movie plot, and I wouldn't have brought it up if it hadn't been important to our subject. So, let me make it more comprehendible.

Souls are genderless energy masses. They are the most intelligent life forms in the universe. They carry the essence of the ever-expanding space and multiply accordingly.

A soul is a Knowledge that is able to multiply by division.

Throughout history, religions have been teaching a variant of this story. Especially that of Christianity. Heaven and Hell come from the physical fact of the karmic weight put on the soul, leaving Earth after spending its lifetime there. Karma accumulates from unsolved issues the human being carries and transmits into the soul as experience, makes it more Earthbound and hinders its exit back to the Shambala when the time arrives. In Christian beliefs, Shambala is Heaven for only karma free, so-called enlightened souls make it. In this sense, Earth is Hell where the heavy souls wander, trapped between the two plains until a Ghostbuster comes to their aid.   There is also a built-in karma cleansing ritual with confession, praying and forgiveness. However, it aims at wiping clean the misconducts, without raising the question of responsibility, therefore not helping the development of the earthling and the soul. This turmoil is always caused by human interactions. The final attempt to lift the load is the Last Sacrament when the earthling has the chance to forgive prior to the end of its life.

Nevertheless, real forgiveness can only come through understanding the fact that everybody is performing 100% of their capability at every given moment. It clears the blame, misconceptions and beliefs surrounding feelings, such as hurt, hate, oppression, neglect and abuse.

Another good example is the case of angels. Apart from the mythology, they arrive into the life of an earthling at birth when an angel appears and starts its laborious task of looking after the newly born. Well, like with everything, it has some truth in it. Souls are helped to maintain macrocosmic connections on the bumpy road of transforming into human beings. They have 2 spirit guides *assigned* to them who provide guidance if asked, or push forward issues when feel necessary. Again, through the eyes of religions they are transformed into guardian angels or my angels. It even comes to a competition when certain people have the idea of being privileged by having these angels while others do not, for according to them, they do not deserve them. And here comes another crucial point, without which life is only a floating existence. Privilege is in the mind, for every earthling is equal. Not the same but equal. Every thought, every sentence and every energy has 2 poles. Today, earthlings talk a lot about equality and work against racism, not realising that all these factors are in the mind. Talking about races establishes their existence, and chisel it into the mind of even the most innocent.

As I mentioned earlier, a soul who wants to descend has the privilege of choosing the background of earthly living. It is due to the fact that reincarnation stopped in 1972, therefore karma doesn't roll over and only souls new to Earth schooling come down here.

Human beings like to think that they choose their children. Many of them pay a substantial amount of money to control gender and the time of birth. It is an illusion to think it possible. Parents only give their genetic appearance, physical structures and certain inclinations in behaviour patterns and inheritable diseases to offspring. They might be able to control the gender of the child with the help of medication, but it very often backfires. As a result, babies are born with confused genders, weak structures and often as disease carriers.

In this sense, a soul in waiting finds a physical body to *jump into*. The gender, the colour of the body, the social background, the family structure and all inheritable illnesses are considered by the incoming soul. This environment produces the soil for growing. The actual jump happens at half term, the moment the foetus moves for the first time. After that, for four and a half months the soul is virtually in the hands of its physical parents and its surroundings. It hears everything, it understands everything, and takes snips of the fragrances around, tastes incoming energies in the form of food, and throughout this time tries hard to maintain the situation.

In the womb the soul becomes used to the physical body, observing its development, learning to use the senses and getting used to the emotions of the environment it chose to grow up in. The experiences of these 18 weeks would give a solid foundation for its earthly life. The balance of new experiences and protection should be established by this point in order to provide the child with curiosity and stamina while letting it gently know that help is always available.

And there is a lot that souls need to get used to. Everything is sort of permanent on Earth. The permanence derives from the necessary usage of the physical body. The body structure itself carries a naturally unchangeable gender that would give a strong direction of living. Surely not many parents–to-be think about the influence gender has on a child's direction. They usually say: *It is better to have a boy first* or *I am so happy it is a girl* or *I would have wanted a boy* or *It is another girl* and I could go on and on. Can you imagine how the child feels hearing these remarks?!

Human beings have children because, according to them, it is the most fulfilling part of life. I emphasize the word *have*. This verb is the source of every misunderstanding, every emotional trauma and every upheaval in life. Ironically every subject in Earth School circles around this word. One doesn't have a child. One gives light, an opportunity for a soul to develop and the possibility for the Self to learn during the process.

We need to establish that everything and everybody is energy and as such has light. Light, that comes from within and faithfully mirrors the current state of the being. The more developed the soul is the more light it projects out and adds to the life force of the planet. Until one day it becomes the light itself. It reaches the state of the ultimate Light that has no Shadow.

The path from a light-bearer to an illuminated person - it is when the soul becomes light - is very bumpy indeed. The first challenge is to learn about the existence of such a path. Like every important thing in life, the path is hidden. Very few talk about it and even less grasp the real meaning. It is a personal Camino. It is an inner journey of self-discovery and development. This road doesn't lead to Santiago de Compostela or any other popular places of pilgrimage that are conveniently serving Christianity. It is a spiritual road, not a religious one. Religions, with their set of beliefs and practices don't provide the freedom to set foot on this path. All religions are codified in one way or another and centred upon moral claims about reality, while the only aim of spirituality is to reach the Source and unite with it. This is the sole task of every earthling.

Now that the Great Cycle of human existence ended, light becomes the centre of attention in every way yet again.

Although I am not going to talk about cycles at large, I think I should mention something about the Great Cycle here. It is the 5 Sun Ages that began 22.250 years ago. The beginning of the first age would coincide with the descent to Atlantis. This cycle ended on the 28th of December 2012 Common Era. It is an astronomical event, or I could say astrological, for modern sciences divided ancient astrology into two separate bases of knowledge and announced astronomy as a science. This was an unfortunate deed, for everything is interrelated and one cannot be viewed without the other. By today we are well into the Golden Era, fighting with the darkness and desperately try to decide the direction we want to take on the evolutionary ladder after the Quantum Leap.

Light as the Fire element comes like Knowledge from above. It is part of the macrocosmic triangle that is getting ready to merge with the microcosmic one.

The Magma, the Fire, the Light, the actual Knowledge in Earth's memory in the centre of the planet is making courageous and drastic movements to connect with the ever-lasting Light of the universe.

Here, I remember a DVD I bought in Uskudar, on the Asian side of Istanbul. It is about the creation from the Muslim point of view. The title *How Allah Created Colours* made me very curious, for it is widely understood that everything we see is an illusion. We do not actually see the object or subject but catch the broken light that mirrored back to us. The lighter the colour and bigger the contrast, the more we can *see*. Our vision of things also depends on the physical structure of our eyes as individuals.

However, the decisive element comes from the mind. When we look at something we only focus with one eye; sometimes with the right and other times with the left. The choice is made by the mind and it greatly depends on the understanding and the inclination of the individual. The right eye notices the physical appearance while the left looks beyond that. Although both send information to the conscious and the subconscious, the final picture is drawn by the mind. We *see* what our mind allows us to see. For example, when a randomly gathered group of people looks at a simple table, some do not even notice its legs, while others notice its style, colour, height, width, but very few would see its energy flow, its energy centres, the worker's energy and the tree it originates from. Let us get back to the DVD now. It is truly beautiful. The message is that nothing has a particular set of colours but the structure and the substance of the object we are looking at, breaks the light in a certain way to send a particular message to the brain making us believe we see colours. This observation carries great sense and coincides with my understanding of life.

I mentioned earlier that everything is interrelated which is why it is not only difficult but rather impossible to focus on these subjects separately. Whatever happens, I promise to get back to the main stream.

From an earthling's point of view we talk about souls and robots living on Earth. To follow the train of thought I elaborate on souls and leave the robots out of the picture.

Knowledge is the data of a particular energy. The word energy derives from the Greek *Energeia* meaning *action, movement*. It is one of those words were mistreated by globalization that transferred its essence to less important meaning. Energy is life itself. Everything that is alive moves. Energy never disappears, it only transforms into different values influenced by the surrounding. I realize that we usually don't talk about energy as a mass. However, every mass centres upon a core that actually gives that particular mass individuality. It is the main data of the mass, the strongest point that carries the characteristics of the whole. According to the data all energy mass has speed, frequency, colour, sound, taste, substance and smell. It also has a polarity that is either positive or negative. Naturally, it doesn't mean good or bad in any way; it is the reigning polarity of the energy.

In the ever-expanding universe everything is energy; either organic or non-organic. One might say dead or alive. The difference between the two is that the organic energy goes through rapid changes, sometimes even self-healing while the alteration in the latter is far slower and more permanent. Planet Earth is an organic energy as is everything that springs out of it.

Regardless of the state, both carry data. Therefore both represent certain knowledge they have acquired during their existence. For example, when I look at my table, I see a dark brown nicely-polished four-legged furniture with a comfortable height and width to cater to my needs at work. I also see an energy with three major energy centres that you might call chakras. Its energy mass that we could call aura, is light green to light bluish in colours with some hint of brown.

When I look further, I see the tree in a forest, near the Nordic Sea, before it was cut out and used for furniture. I could tap into each level of the procedure and would be able to talk about the life of the workers, the company, the designer, the store and the transporter. This information, this data is the knowledge of my table, and makes up its energy field. On the other hand, when I look at my next-door neighbour Aida, on top of the usually-observed features I see an energy mass with seven major chakras showing her general physical and emotional state with the momentary situation added to it. The general state is made up of the past lives on Earth, karma and unfinished businesses while the momentary would tell me if she is in a good mood or not, and the way she feels about the world at the given time. This knowledge about her would come to me mostly through sounds and colours with additional help from other senses.

With our limited understanding, we see life as the cycle of the microcosm that is Earth, rather than being part of the greater cycle of the macrocosm that is the universe.

According to the ancient Egyptians, there was the very first dot one would call the Creator Force. By time, the dot projected itself out to become 2 dots next to each other. After endless projections the dots made up a line. It is a very good way of grabbing the essence of creation, particularly because we look at everything as 2 dimensional. I go a bit further and say that the first dot went through certain experiences reached the highest evolutionary level, the crystallized Knowledge and became the Source.

"Life is a constant cycle of searching for personal truth"

AKIA-PATH-FINDER 2

THE CONTRACT

Before descending to Earth, a soul goes through an evaluation of its abilities, and the aim is set and summed up in a contract as a constant reminder. Like with everything, it is good and bad. It is good for keeping the soul on track in a form of intuition or as a bouncer that is triggered every time the aim is lost. It is bad for the same reason, for without walking the side roads, experiencing is limited and the filters in the mind stop valuable addition to the thoughts for future use on the path to fulfilment.

The contract is one of life's greatest mysteries and a bottomless well of mental and emotional disorders.

It is one of the most decisive conditions in evaluating and achieving the highest level of contentment and the best possible living conditions in earthly existence. Without understanding them, individuals go astray or find their heads hitting thick brick walls, seem to appear from nowhere, hindering their desires to reach certain destinations. Then, in an attempt to remedy the situation certain courses are taken on reaching the goals you set out for yourself, change your life, achieve greatness, and become a millionaire and so on. Others would succumb to the inevitable, announcing that fate caught up with them and there is nothing else to be done. Again, like with everything both approaches have a firm ground to stand on.

Yes, there are events human beings cannot change, not after initiating it that is. One of them is the contract. And yes, there are changeable events. However, the understanding of this phenomenon requires a high level of special intelligence. Please follow the motto:

> *God, give me the serenity*
> *to accept the things, I cannot change.*
> *Courage, to change the things I can,*
> *And wisdom always to see the difference.*

The origin of this wisdom is not clearly known. It has been in circulation for hundreds of years. My earliest encounter with a similar concept was through an ancient Egyptian script, dating back around 4 thousand years. Nevertheless, its best-known appearance was on the wall of the main character in Kurt Vonnegut's Slaughterhouse 5. Check it out, if you have the chance.

These 2 sentences are special keys to Knowledge. I have them on the wall in the study as a special reminder. After all, I am a human being too, and my life is just as challenging. Let's get back to the possible outcomes of ignoring the contract.

Similarly to everyday practice, this contract is *signed* binding the bearer to follow certain behaviour patterns and stay within the dotted lines. It is far more psychological than legal. While in earthly living a contract wears off after the event or period of time is passed, and the punishment for breaking it is decided by other human beings in the court of law, this *document* is in place, as it was intended, for the whole lifetime, lurking in the background, reminding you of the promises you made to none other than yourself. Therefore, there is no human power or amount of money that can free you from it, and the punishment is set by your standard and values of life.

Let me elaborate on this thought. Don't take it the wrong way. There is nothing bad about having money. However, the why, how and for what are the decisive questions.

Money, the new God is used for providing escape routes out of contracts, either verbal or written. It eases or totally demolishes responsibilities that are greatly required for understanding interactive existence and living as part of the human community. Although, there is a force, pushing wealthy people towards sharing and goodwill, however, it runs on the surface and gets thinner over time. Attracting media popularity overrides personal challenges in the eyes of many. Most of the charities are money-making schemes with hidden disruptive purposes rather than helping the poor and needy. I only want to add one sentence here: poverty is the requirement of wealth. The greater the poverty, the higher the wealth, for the gap between the 2 creates the value of each. They are the 2 ends of the same stick.

Think about it! Having 1,000 USD wouldn't take you farther than a week or two in a so-called rich country but you can comfortably live on it in a poorer one for a few months. It means that having money where everybody has, will not make you rich, and will not provide you with a shallow satisfaction of being successful. Nevertheless, none of the above mentioned schemes would override the contract you *signed* with the soul that became the part of you in the process of becoming an earthling.

Since the purpose of humanity is to help the soul's evolutionary process, this contract might not embrace the most favourable living conditions, for solving challenges are needed for spiritual growth. This work cannot be delegated or bought by money, for it would enhance the employee rather than the employer.

"Live without bringing shame on yourself"

AKIA-PATH-FINDER 3

THE SPIRIT GUIDES

As I mentioned earlier, spirit guides are usually referred to as guardian angels due to modern Christian views. Unfortunately, these alterations made the otherwise flawless knowledge very confusing. Let's start with the name: Christianity. Christo, is a Greek word, meaning enlightened. It is not a name and not unique to any of the prophets or any person. It was given to earthlings who reached a high level of esoteric knowledge, as a distinguisher. However, the religion didn't recognise the knowledge related to the universe, put its chosen prophet on a pedestal and adding Christo to its given name.

Pre-Old-Testament groups, we usually refer to as Pagans, used Christo for their most knowledgeable. History embraces them as early Christians, however, neither their philosophy nor their understanding of nature and life bore similarities to that of the religion.

Following this event, the communication with the universe was placed into the jurisdiction of the Church and people ended up with guardian angels. They are out of the world beings and said to take care of earthlings who are chosen for the privilege, as the result of their behaviour and commitment to the Church.

Before you start feeling rejected, neglected or chosen – by the way, none of them are healthy – I need to tell you that privilege only exists in the minds of earthlings. Human beings judge according to their mental and emotional intelligence. Doesn't matter which way they go, they end up in the category they value more. Guarding and guiding are two, totally different approaches. The first would take care of the subject regardless, removing the caution and responsibilities while the latter would provide insight and help in decision making if needed and requested. Spirit guides are not caretakers.

The confusion is furthered when earthlings, again mostly Christians, lend somewhat human form to these angels by replacing them with departed relatives, usually grandparents.

The older generation always has a special place in the hearts of earthlings. They are not the responsible and disciplinary caretakers, only see them on special occasions therefore, their emotions towards the youngsters appear more genuine and nearer to love, the unconditional acceptance we all seek.

Clairvoyance is one of the great abilities of earthlings. It is a French word that translates into seeing clearly. The degree of this capability depends on the spiritual intelligence of the individual human being. However, it is impossible to see something that one cannot imagine existing. I have worked for the most prominent psychic platforms and have been teaching the art for years. It is fascinating to gauge the development of my students as they are advancing in their studies, and I found it equally interesting how colleagues with limited viewpoints on life were only able to convey the fragment of the message sent.

The physical eye – not the third eye, the collective sense – takes in the rays of light that bounce back from the object. The image perceived ends up in the conscious and the subconscious for proper evaluation. The first, we usually refer to as logic and the latter as emotions. Well, none of it is true. However, since we do not understand emotions very much, and we know equally limited of the subconscious, we put them into the same basket for convenience. Psychic abilities, such as seeing, hit everybody at certain stages of life. Earthlings are born with their third eye open, however, it usually *closes* due to the influences of narrow-minded adults and the media. It doesn't really close, merely refuses to see or allows only partial function. I am certain you went through experiences when entering a room with a group and you all come back with different experiences. Some see the furniture, the colour of the walls and others would pick up life-changing clues.

Like with everything else, seeing needs to be learned consciously. It is not only about psychic ability but also the everyday usage of the senses. There are 3 levels of seeing according to spiritual experience.

1. Mantic images

These images depict basic psychic abilities when the individual either lacks imagination or due to fear, dresses the visions up to resemble lost relatives, imaginary figures, favourite or feared characters, depending on the momentary state of mind. Teaching and warnings would usually come from grandparents, and destructive thought would be delivered by the devil. There would be a familiar smile on grandma's face and her clothing, sometimes even her fragrance would bring reassurance of her presence. The devil would definitely wear black, half man half animal with red horns and a grim face, as it has been depicted throughout the ages. At this stage of seeing, mantic images are like dreams.

The dressing up of thoughts and psychic sightings mirror the mental and emotional understanding of the bearer.

2. Telesmatic images

These images are built deliberately, although usually subconsciously, by the creative power of thoughts. They come to existence when a buffer zone is needed to make life more bearable or understandable. We use them for altering the past, the reality of the present or drawing the future.

Earthlings hang onto their suffering more than joyful events, and they want to justify this pain. People, on the other side of the fence become dark villains, lending emphasis to the anguish.

Over time, the camp of the villains gets bigger as new individuals are added to it. In this dormant state, telesmatic images are like fantasies, used for creating new realities supporting chosen lifestyles and ways of thinking.

Long existing thoughtforms, such as voluntary beliefs, are also telesmatic images and they produce visions accordingly.

The state of telesmatic images is somewhere on the second half of the long road towards enlightenment. However, the lack of consciousness and courage holds earthlings back from reaching the goal that is conscious clarity. And this is the sole root of mental and emotional disorders, such as depression, empathy, anxiety, fear and insecurity. It is the state where ignorance is left but enlightenment hasn't reached. As you know, ignorance is bliss. It really is. Nothing and nobody can hurt you there. You cannot feel the troops marching on your back, for you don't know of their existence. On the other hand, in the state of illumination, comprehending the difference between changeable and constant empowers you with the courage of taking a step forward. Therefore nothing and nobody can hurt you there either. Your safety is in your knowledge.

Look at life! We are all familiar with the phenomenon of giving up midterm. The start offers the excitement of the new and learning. However, depending on the mental and emotional intelligence of the earthling involved, the stage arrives when progress becomes harder and achievements have fewer appearances. It is the time when frustration sets in and takes away all the remaining courage. Fear of failing or even succeeding sets in and confuses the thoughts. The road becomes blurry and the mind is trapped.

This entrapment requires the help of a consciously enlightened aide.

Many of these telesmatic images are drawn from the collective consciousness. They are much stronger than self-creations. That is how brainwashing works for they can become very strong and live as existing part of life.

3. Phosphoric images

They are the sign of attainment. They occur when a carefully built telesmatic image draws its energy from the universe, becomes a bridge and later a physical reality. The energy comes from within when the inner light beams through the image.

Every soul, living on Earth has a set of 2 spirit guides. Not more, not less. The number of them doesn't change in any circumstances. The first pair is assigned to earthlings at birth, and works with them until detectable spiritual advancement. Then, like in schools, a new set of guides step in to take the human being to the next level of knowledge.

The knowledge I am mentioning is linked to the matrix where the interrelations of energies are explained and the birth-right capabilities developed. However, spirit guides are ready to give advice on everyday earthly matters also. Their messages come in a form of intuition, or better yet, a one-to-one meeting can be set up to discuss matters near to heart.

Nevertheless, I want to clarify that guides are guiding. You cannot assign chores to them, and they do not take care of you. Life is yours, to win. Your spirit guides are ready to push you into the finishing line.

Spirit guides are souls who once lived on Earth therefore they fully understand the challenges a human being may encounter here. They are also excellent astral traveller, change dimensions with ease and above all, their knowledgebase is ready to be picked at any time you feel the need for it. They usually appear in the form they last lived on this planet.

Meeting your guides is not dangerous. Sit down in a room, alone. Light 2 long white candles during the time of the full moon. Extinguish all artificial lighting. Make yourself comfortable and chant: *I am ready to meet my guides.*

Keep an open mind and do not get scared. You don't need to see the moon while you are doing it. Night time is better for the senses to be sharper. The full moon opens communication gateways for the guides to get in touch with you. Look at the flickering candlelight while repeating the mantra. Mirroring your spiritual awareness, after a while, you will feel a sensation of a presence and communication is established.

"You must remake yourself in the eternity of your body"

AKIA-PATH-FINDER 4

THE FAMILY

A family is a group of people held together by expectations, roleplay, and fear. A family doesn't need to have blood relations. The DNA connection only applies to the physical body of a human being and sits in the minds of those who are stuck on the limited plain of reality. In order to explain the emotional and mental structure of a family, we need to open the horizon towards the universe.

Everything is interrelated in the whole, ever-expanding universe. The biggest mistake earthlings do is that they want to explain planet Earth and humanity as separate entities. This way assumptions are made and stories invented to fill in the gaps. Looking back in history, none of the popular stories stands ground. The universe is like the perfect ashlar in the alchemical concept.

It might be a good time to let you know that against all fashionable beliefs, alchemy originates from Egyptian teachings, hence the name Al Khemi. Khem is the name of ancient Egypt and the expression means the Matter of Khem. I do not want to follow this lead further because I would never stop talking about it, and the purpose of this book demands me to get back on track. Therefore, let us leave it as it is for now. Nevertheless, the perfect ashlar still requires some clarification. With this thought, we need to travel back to the beginning of Freemasonry. As it is with all the clear Knowledge, it was totally distorted over time, fell victim to gap-filling stories and explanations, and became the prominent agent for the power struggle of The New World Order. That is why we need the root.

Embracing the harmony within the interrelations of energies, in the beginning, these masons were commissioned to build important sanctuaries and centres, manipulating the energies of nature by their knowledge of The Matrix. Their symbol was the perfect ashlar, the stone wall, constructed from uneven and rough-surfaced rocks, fit together in such a fashion that was able to provide a strong base for enormous buildings and withstand time. The most peculiar nature of the perfect ashlar is that the rocks are placed together without filling or added glue material. This way the organic energy flow within the construction is harmonious hence follows the matrix. This is what metaphysics is all about; putting genuine structures together and discarding the non-related speculations. Al Khemi is the teaching of metaphysics, the interrelations of energies in the universe, including Earth and earthlings.

It shouldn't be a big shock that earthlings arrived at the planet from the universe. The lack of a valid link between the DNA structure of the animal kingdom and humans serves as an explanation. This is an important factor we need to embrace.

There are basically two types of earthlings in existence: souls and robots. Neither of them is better than the other one, only different. The metamorphosis lies in the structure of the mind. Earthlings that are the amalgamated result of a soul and a physical body, remember. In their subconscious, they carry the Knowledge from the universe, while robots embrace only earthly experiences through the conscious.

The family is life's biggest playground, where members continue or start learning the interrelations of events. It is the place for not only mental but also emotional development: the beginning of the journey towards emotional intelligence.

As the greatest play that is written as lived, family life is the most influential education to which an earthling has access. They can learn about leadership or the lack of it, the effects of emotional manipulation, and the struggle for respect or just being heard. In a conscious family, members are equal however, remain within their elected roles, always keeping in mind the prosperity of the unit through the spiritual education of individuals. I want to remind you here that spiritual education has nothing to do with religion. It is the enriching power of understanding and working towards the enlightenment on the purpose of existence.

I do not want to go far back in history, why and when the family concept was created because it is irrelevant to our task here. The most important is to establish that the smallest nucleus in human society serves as an imaginary shield against the biggest enemy of mankind: fear. It also serves as an easily manipulated unit in capitalist money-making schemes.

Fear comes from a lack of knowledge or information. They fear the dark because they cannot see what is there, and do not have the working ability to use other senses. The fear of water comes from not being able to swim well enough to conquer its power. The fear in an abusive relationship mirrors the incapacity of leaving the environment. These are examples of the lack of trust in the Self that is a major issue in the matrix of the family structure. The primary duty of the parents is to plant the understanding of responsibility into the minds of their children and cultivate their confidence and capabilities to conquer life's challenges. If a grownup person – I would say around 21 years of age in today's civilization – doesn't have a strong enough desire to fly out of the nest and set up existence on their own, life would become more and more diluted and slowly fades away; unless an outside influence opens a gate towards conscious living. It also shows a lack of consistency in parenting skills.

The basic subjects of this floating illusion varied throughout the ages, reflecting the overall feelings of societies and human groups living side by side. Today, these feelings are strongly manipulated by the interwoven media that serves the desires of the power clusters, fast closing up on humanity.

In the 21st century, the new god Money is ruling, and the lack of it put a lot of strain on couples, families and earthlings in general. Interestingly enough, people with some money are far more stressed than those not having any. Providing for the self and the dependants on a daily basis is in alignment with nature. However, money is not tangible, therefore having it creates an even stronger fear of losing it. The feeling is valid. Due to its liquid state, it can evaporate at any time and without excuse. The struggle for survival is created by political and financial institutions to validate their work and make the most from people in the process.

Many earthlings feel that politics are unimportant when we talk about their mental and spiritual welfare. They cannot be more mistaken. Everything they do, they eat, they think, they say, they wear and work with, is politics, and support the beliefs of the major political and financial groups. This support means that they permit them to act on their behalf without continuously demanding an explanation for their moves. Unconsciously they give away control over their existence.

Depending on the level of consciousness and relation with life and fellow earthlings, they might finally realize what is happening, and start making noises, usually to themselves at first, and to the family later. The latter is very tricky indeed. Due to the absence of consciousness, there are not many families, where you can openly discuss different political, sexual and ethical views, without losing face and respect, or being subjected to some kind of mockery. These conversations, or the lack of them, put a strong impact on the lives, especially the future of the members concerned.

Where there are two earthlings, one of them is the leader. Even in partnerships. One of them will make the final decision. It is valid for families also. The role is not necessarily taken by the member with the highest level of intelligence but by the strongest. Sometimes traditions set the rules about this structure. There are many families today where children are ruling. Again, this behaviour shows weak parenting skills and I really feel sorry for the children.

Although scientific researches cannot prove the continuous DNA chain between animals and humans, the media is hooked on this concept. They are also hanging onto the theory that there was the first human couple, created by some kind of humanlike supernatural power, who started to populate Earth. Interestingly enough, these totally different ideas seem to meet somewhere and produce an amalgamated concept that earthlings originate from Adam's rib while still fit into the evolutionary pattern.

This is the greatest paradox of the family foundation. The two ideas can only go hand in hand in an unconscious mind, for both are floating in the air without any tangible substance. I do not want to get into the metaphysics of creation here, for it is not the purpose of this particular book.

However, I need to touch upon certain beliefs to help understand the metaphysical concept of the family. Stating that Adam was the all-power mirror of the almighty concept, paved the axiomatic status that females are inferior to males. The thought is strengthened by the much ruling Christian idea of the Trinity, where all three presences are males. The metaphysical - and the original - concept of the Trinity shows the two poles – depicted as a male and a female - that is in everything, work together, help each other to climb the ladder of evolution by creating the balance of the two poles within, to achieve the highest greatness possible. This quality improvement is symbolised by the child, as the new beginning of a more intelligent life, guided by its parents on the road of experiencing and learning.

The concept of the metaphysical understanding is that every human being is equal but not the same. Regardless of your origin, you have the same opportunities to achieve greatness. The emphasised understanding is that personal achievement is not measured by material wealth.

With this statement, we've arrived at an extremely delicate understanding of earthly living and family values.

The first thought we need to familiarise ourselves with is that parents do not own their children. People have offspring for different reasons however, only one is valid. It is a way to test and put forward existing experiences and gain new ones. It is also a lesson in responsibility and understanding unconditional love. I feel weird to put an adjective in front of love because love is unconditional. I'd like to clarify here that loving your children unconditionally doesn't mean that you mastered the greatness of the art for you placed a condition on your feelings, and this condition is that they are your children. However, like everything important, it is hard to follow. Earthlings make excuses and invent expressions, ideas and boxes to fit their capabilities and desire. They usually use the main word as the umbrella. Today we hear about motherly love, fatherly love, friendly love, passionate love and so on but none of them is unconditional, therefore not love. Love is neutral. It means that regardless of what others do, love is theirs. Due to insecurity, fear and lack of emotional intelligence, it is a mighty hard task for earthlings. Nevertheless, the easiest ground for practice is the parents – children's connection.

Earthlings are responsible for their deeds, words, and thoughts. This duty also covers the behaviour they should adopt towards their children.

It is the parents' choice to have additions to the family and it makes their responsibility to look after them until they grow into adulthood. Interestingly in societies where having children might not be much of a choice due to life's values or religion, people tempt to look after their offspring and unconditional love is understood more than in places where the option is given. The second very important thought in the metaphysical structure of the family we need to understand is that children are not the extension of their parents. They might take on some of their habits and way of thinking however, it has more to do with observations or subconscious learning than genetics. In Western societies, many people go through much heartache and physical suffering to produce children they could call their own. In the so-called lesser civilised world it is understood that children are precious and also the fact that they need fathering and mothering guidance and attention, rather than a set of people they are related to by DNA.

I am certain you have observed that children of the same couple and similar upbringing, turn out to be totally different from one another. It is due to the fact that under the DNA skin there are souls with individual heritage and adaptability. Without understanding this concept, lives can totally fall apart within the family structure.

The third is that parents are not servants or slaves to their children. They should have a life to handle and aims to pursue. However, their responsibility is to teach values to their children. It is important to look at each member as an individual human being rather than from the relation's point of view.

Earthly living is a school where human beings are faced with challenges to help evolve. One of them is to live and work in a family structure. The responsibility dictates, that on the road to achieving greatness, the members need to help each other in finding the self, first of all. This act requires the basic understanding that everybody is working towards the same aim of self-discovery, and despite the role within the unit, there is no such thing as a perfect human being, for flows and merits are essential parts of human nature. Teaching is done by learning. It is also true the other way around. By understanding and embracing this concept, shame and fear would fade and constructive energy would gain a prominent place in one's life.

"The night is not the end of a bad day but the beginning of a better one"

AKIA-PATH-FINDER 5

THE CODE

The code is all the permanent or hopefully semi-permanent dogmas, rules, regulations, moral standards, ways of thinking and understanding a human being carries. It is unique to every person. As life goes by, more experience is gained that either loosens or tightens the existing management system of The Mind.

Social media is flooded by articles, books and advertisements from meditation centres, self-claimed healers and coaches who talk about the permanence of codes, something that is unchangeable, carried from the ancestors through seven generations. I do not support the idea. The trodden path of the grandparents is a lively learning ground. However, this view will transfer the lineage's responsibility for their deeds, onto your shoulders, creating quite an upheaval and many obstacles in life. When we look at the constantly moving Universe we realize that this idea is only wishful thinking by those who dislike change and dwell in the past. Or of those who want to implant fear and with that, a total succumb to man-made controlling rules. It is a dangerous idea indeed. The foundation is fragile and totally dismisses the possibility of the Macrocosm by turning Earthlings into narrow-minded robot-like creatures with limited choices about the future. Only a few realise that by taking on the codes of the parents, the weight of whole humanity will be shifted on their existence. It is a chain that is traceable back to the beginning. You take on your mother's code while she is already having her mother's. Your grandmother also has her mother's and so on. So actually you are carrying the responsibility, karma and codes of the whole 22,000 odd years of earthly living. I cannot figure out why people are playing with the 7 generation idea. It is so unreal. When you arrive at the 7th ancestors, you already covered 21,844 persons, and how would you know or how would anybody know which of the deeds, thoughts or words of the 16,384 ancestors in the 7th generations you are responsible for? Following this theory, these people also have the responsibility for their ancestors so you need to separate those that only belong to them. But how can you do that? All our decisions are influenced by others, our ancestors included. Such a mess!

This theory is a consciously built machinery to keep you feeling guilty for everything humanity has ever done to help its decline. The wars, mass killing, colonisation and wiping off nature. Not to mention the crimes committed against the self. Many people follow or relive the life of a parent of the same gender believing that there is no choice; that this path has to be taken for it is karmic or simply fate. Well, choices do not come to you by themselves. One needs to have adequate information to be presented with choices, find the path to them and learn to embrace the presented possibilities. For many people having choices is a curse. Different aspects need to be looked at, and decisions have to be made. Work with the changes, fear of the unknown would push these people back into their comfort zone.

There are certain cases when one follows the footsteps of a parent without much thought and consideration, and when reality hits it is too late to stop the motion. Looking at parents as role models can make or break the future of a child. There is far more to parenting than staying together and pretending to be a happy family. There are also physical inclinations such as certain movements and ways of carrying oneself; likes and dislikes for food, drink, events and so on. As likes and dislikes are in the mind, I would not take them for codes. My parents divorced when I was 4 years old. I lived with my mother who was constantly blaming my father for every mishap and every pain and told nasty stories about him, even though she was already remarried and had a new baby from the second marriage. One day, when I was eating sourcrout, which happened to be my very favourite dish, she mentioned that I was a lot like my father because I loved the dish and so did he. I put the spoon down straight away and had not looked at a sour cabbage dish for a couple of years until I had the opportunity to meet my father and understand him a bit better. I realized that he was a good person so it stopped bothering me that I was in any way like him.

Biological inclinations are very tricky indeed. The physical body is the merge of 2 other bodies – your parents - therefore there is a great possibility to develop inclinations towards certain illnesses, strengths or weaknesses, carried by one of the merging bodies.

These tendencies are dormant until key energy triggers them open. And here we arrive back to the interrelations of energies, for it is the key to everything. Depending on the relationship between conscious and subconscious, one carries a certain emotional state which works as a magnet and pulls in similar energies to interfere with the condition of the existing one. This is how inclinations open and blend into the life of the unsuspecting victim. There is also a time when lessons should be learned, such as blaming your mother for something, and life presents you with a similar situation to make you understand that whatever she did, it was the result of a simple fact, that she didn't know better.

There is another expression earthling like to use as a shield and a sound excuse for not doing life-related chores, and it is Fate. Similarly to the code, it is deemed inheritable and unchangeable. It is neither. Learning and changing are not prohibited.

Every day I meet someone who would state that life is all suffering. Loneliness, physical and mental hardship are the companions. However, nothing to be done. It is fate. Usually, they say that the suffering is to offer redemption for an ancestor who stepped over a few lines and became an outsider of the law. These individuals look upon themselves as The Good Ones. They cannot be further from it. Since we live in interrelations they poison the existence of the rest of the population also. Through their behaviour they force others to accept their viewpoint. If you think about it, it is a selfish act. They do not help anybody, only destroy.

I have been teaching the highest level of Alchemy, classic Witchcraft, Orixa, Voudoun, Tarot, and other nature-related Wisdom, so I am not bashing the existence of outside forces. However, they are part of the whole, just like you are. Also part of The Knowledge earthlings should acquire. They are only supernatural if the folder is labelled that way. Leave your fear behind and invite them into your conscious to add a fascinating extension to life. You need to be careful though. Find a good master, who doesn't feed you with imaginary non-sense and tells you that one has to be born with the ability to understand and work with these forces. Remember, every earthling carries The Knowledge in The Pineal Gland. So do you.

"The outside knowledge is the key to the wisdom within"

AKIA-PATH-FINDER 6

THOUGHTS

The impulses in the mind are all organic energies carrying data that have been altered by effects and counter effects, helping or hindering the owner. If the management is good the result would tilt towards the helping end.

The *everything is interrelated*, slogan offers ample space to endless, the untouchable and unimaginable quantity of information, and their explanations. Without proper understanding this bounty could lead to an extremely dangerous way of thinking. In this aspect the beginning, the end, and the middle are vague, for every end is the beginning of something, and also the middle of another happening.

As an explanation, I would like to start with my beginning. Since this beginning was chosen by my mind, it is not at all illegal to oppose it. However, my choice sets boundaries to the train of my ideas, loosens or tightens their living space.

The loosening and the tightening, as the choice of the beginning, foremost depend on the momentary state of my mind, on my relation to the subject, and the goal in front of my eyes. The information I have, my knowledge, my scruples, my upbringing, my schooling, my social background, my pledges, and my conscience, also play a decisive role in my deed. They all, and many more little ingredients send certain passwords to the brain to test and try the key into the locks of neatly filed folders, and into those laying around in lazy untidiness. This action happens in support of the strongest impulse, meaning the most urgent and most important task in the mind, waiting to be solved. If I am lucky, one of the keys would fit into a lock and I would find few refreshing and helping thoughts behind the door.

Regardless of being conscious - formed under pressure - or subconscious - finds its way without invitation - after creation, the thought becomes an organic energy mass. Imagine it, like the cartoons where the drawn figures' thoughts are being written in a little, balloon-like surface with an end pointing towards the person that masterminded it. This particular Earthling would be the starting point of the thought-energy.

In the universe everything is energy and they follow the rule of *likes attract*. It is true for thought forms also. By popping out of the brain, the thought would become alive. Like all other organic energy forms, the thought would start needing something to feed on. The pointed end turns around and searches for nourishment. This search is guided by the energy of the thought, meaning the words written on the balloon. The natural choice would be the person for whom it was intended. In the hope of reaching it on time, the thought starts its feverish search for the addressee. When found, the thought-form will hook onto a similar energy and make itself heard.

However, if the energy of that person has a different frequency, the thought turns and goes back to the sender. Telepathy and cursing follow the same structure. It means that telepathy only works between two persons with similar frequency and a curse only works with people who have inclination towards it.

Let me put it into practice! You broke up with your partner and you are not happy about it. It is the time when you forget about unconditional love and in your thoughts, you wish them loneliness and torture for the rest of their life. The thought-form you have created is a low frequency, slow energy. To find a comfortable base with the addressee, they need to be similarly unhappy and miserable. If it is not the case, the thought will come back and torment you further. This scenario is set in a fairly clear background. However with the cyber debris, SMS-s, emails, phone calls, and the countless thoughts popping out of people's heads all over the place, one needs to be a master energy manipulator to go through the obstacles they create for a thought-form.

It has been said that thoughts don't count. And words or deeds are far more important.

Remember that the strength of both lies in the power of mental creation.

THE MIND

The more you understand, the happier you'll be, because it is all in the mind.

As the philosophy, that observes and teaches the interrelation between the unseen soul and the cosmic knowledge, **AKIA** gives you free hands to discover and open the depth of the Universe and the mind.

In everyday living Earthlings go through traumas, mishaps, joy, happiness, pleasure, hatred, envy, devilishness, fear, sadness, pain, love and other controversial emotions, and not many of them understand that all their deeds and feelings actually spring from the mind.

The Mind is a management centre, where the data - that is stored in the filing cabinet, called Brain - is processed.

In the metaphysical understanding, the mind of a soul - flesh amalgamated earthling has 4 compartments. Each is assigned to one of the 4 basic elements that we all contain in the physical body. These are as follows:

- ❖ The Conscious – *Earth element*
- ❖ The Subconscious – *Water element*
- ❖ The Ego – *Air element*
- ❖ The Pineal Gland – *Fire element*

As we already established, everything is interrelated. Therefore elaborating on one point will open all the avenues eventually. However, this book has a certain goal, therefore I need to cut the side roads short. If you would like to know more about the effects of the elements, please visit akiaphilosophy.com.

In the case of the mind, **The Pineal Gland** is the starting point, the 0000 as Sheldon would say in the Big Bang Theory. It contains the untouched, perfect structure of the universe, and since everything is interrelated, it is axiomatic that this format is the key to all creations within. Folders in **The Pineal Gland** contain The Akashic Records of planets and souls. These are pure numeric translations of energy substances, untouched by mankind, or anybody else, as the matter of fact. When certain evolutionary states are reached, the data slowly makes its way into **The Subconscious** for further assistance.

It is said by few, that **The Pineal Gland** is The Third Eye. I totally disagree with that. However, like with everything, there is some truth in this belief. The first contains all the Knowledge and the second is constantly sharpened to seek the Knowledge. The Third Eye is the Sixth Sense that is capable of using all the five together. Naturally, it can only happen if the basic understanding of *everything is energy* is set in. Using the five senses, The Third Eye goes beyond the abilities of each one, and sees, hears, tastes, senses, smells all at once. This way a far more accurate picture of the object is drawn.

There are others, who would urge you to cleanse **The Pineal Gland.** Please, stay away from it. It might be the very last extraordinary gift of nature that human beings haven't destroyed yet. It is a storage place, one needs to learn keywords to enter into and respect to use.

The Subconscious stores the data leaked over from **The Pineal Gland**. Unsorted impulses and emotional experiences from this life also land there.

The Conscious is the place where the clarified files live, representing the actual Knowledge of the owner. It is the Wisdom gained through experiences in this lifetime, ready to be added to everyday practice.

The Ego is the filing manager. Teachings, usually coming from the Far-East, pushing you to lose your ego and become nothing, are agents of the New World Order. Without your **Ego**, you do not live. Having said that, its purpose and structure need clarifications.

I would say, **The Ego** is your darker side that challenges you daily where new information or experience is concerned. It is your fear that holds you back. Nevertheless, getting rid of it is not the solution. Take the tests and win them. The clearer the data in your mind, the better it is for the knowledge. For example, in the back of your head, that is **The Subconscious**, you have certain feelings that there is more to living than what you understand. **The Ego** would say, *no no, there is nothing there!* Your right answer would be a *challenge is accepted* and start digging.

The filing system in your mind is your business, **The Ego** is your employee. If it gets confused about your position and unclear instructions, it will overwrite you and take the lead. As in every business, it would be a disaster, for one of you has to assume responsibility.

Let us take an everyday event through the process of the mind.

You walk on the street and you see someone smiling at you as you pass them by. The impulse triggers your mind straight away and starts generating thoughts that mirror your evolutionary state, your knowledge, and your understanding. **The Conscious** and **The Subconscious** will create images of the person. If you are a comfort zone being, who is content with life within, you might not even notice the subconscious data, for the filing manager will not emphasise it. However, even though we like the comfort zone, from time to time most of us allow the purpose of life – experience and learning - shine through from **The Pineal Gland**, into **The Subconscious**, and manifest in dreams, desires, and fantasies. With the creative power of thoughts, desire and reality produce an amalgamated version of the event that, will win the centre stage of the mind. The more you know about life, energies, behaviours and other human beings, the more colourful and accurate the picture becomes. Desires and fantasies are living products of your creative power, therefore you need mental clarity to correctly handle them. Without understanding the borders between the faculties of the mind, confusion sets, **The Matrix** disappears, and the structure collapses. Remember, you need to hang onto **The Matrix**. The interrelations are keys to living. You are in control. Do not believe that thoughts are just coming to your mind from nowhere, and regardless of what you do, four thousands of them are tormenting you in every given moment, until the end. These thoughts are the product of loose ends and miscellaneous files that do not fit into any folders, or the filing manager is doing a poor job. Either way, it is your call to put them right.

Thoughts of any kind need to be monitored and sorted. Major clearance twice a year will do a good job of tidying them. Discard those that do not fit. Fantasies should remain within the boundaries of plausible. I am not suggesting that you need to hold yourself back. However, idle dreams take up space and energy therefore, there is no point in keeping them alive.

As you are gaining new experiences on a daily basis, you add new files to the existing ones in your filing cabinet. When connections are cleared, a folder is created to hold them together. Then it is taken into account as part of **The Conscious**, adding to **The Wisdom.**

Examples of these folders are *Work, Dwelling, Property, School,* and *Health.* They manage their everyday existence based upon the experiences filed.

The greatest challenge to the filing system of **The Conscious** is presented by the Media. The vast majority of the powerful people in the media are ignorant about metaphysics, wisdom and knowledge therefore, their contribution would add to the clusters rather than to the useful. However, since you are the boss, you need to recognise it and instruct **The Ego** accordingly. The folders in **The Subconscious**, such as *Past lives, Present, Future, Soul Siblings, Tasks, and Contracts* are parts of the essential information, ready to be discovered, and used as the knowledge, the wisdom that helps with endeavours, on the path, of becoming a better human being, in the sense of unity and wholeness. They offer solutions to everyday mental dysfunctions and psychological disorders. There is also one file, has *Miscellaneous* scrabbled on the front, with an indescribable hue of pink. It stores runaway files that, sort of limber undecidedly between **The Conscious** and **The Subconscious**.

As an example, let us look at the first folder titled *Past lives*. It stores the data of one's ancestors as a soul, the soul-number, the basic abilities, the soul-codes, works the soul accomplished, events it passed through, experiences it had, battles it conquered or lost, and most importantly the knowledge that the soul collected during its lives, prior to the one it struggles with or enjoys here, as an amalgamation with physical attributes, down on this wonderful planet, called Earth. Although it brings more responsibility, learning is the essence of life, one needs to take to the road towards the greatest challenge of all, Happiness.

"Wisdom is knowledge you can make use of"

AKIA-PATH-FINDER 7

RELATIONSHIPS

Everything, what and who we are, is invested
into the most important interrelations of all,
human interactions.

In today's lonely world, there are many of us
finding consolation in the company of animals.
However, it is an unequal position, for
conversation is limited and your pet is at your
mercy. It is a hideaway from responsibilities and
challenges. Loneliness comes from within and
having any kind of company is not going to
change this fact, only conceals it.

Like everything, human interactions are boxed
for convenience. We talk about family relations,
friendships, colleagues, work connections,
buddies, and romantic interests and so on. There
seems to be some kind of protocol that states
how and what within each package. When you
are rude to your mother, she would remind you
that she wasn't your buddy, and when giving
advice to the latter, you would get the, *you are*

not my mother phrase. Your boss doesn't want to be treated like your colleagues and your romantic relationship demands more than your friends. These settings are the parts of the never-ending and always changing scenes on the stage of life. From the metaphysical point of view, all labels belong to the same game.

Each of these boxes would grow into a comfort zone over time. The initial purpose of joining the groups will fade as the feeling of belonging gets stronger. You would learn to navigate within and between them. Making compromises, the ability to give in, lobbying for recognition and leadership grow into valued weapons in your survival kit. Regardless of the status within a certain group, every member is fighting for acknowledgement. The chosen weapon mirrors the emotional intelligence of the warrior and the target. These battles are usually taken for emotional attachments.

When your mother is silently slaving for you, doing your laundry, cleaning your room, cooking and handling all the chores, she is struggling with her low self-esteem as a human being and aiming for some kind of recognition, she might label as love, from the universe. You will take her approach as a duty or affection. However, nobody, not even the universe respects quiet slaves. This behaviour is against progressive human nature and there is no way it helps either of the two involved. If she makes a lot of noise while performing those acts, then she is definitely in need of praises, and she'd like to see you by her side in the parental power-struggle. When your father buys you the latest iPhone and pays for your amusements, it is compensation for not taking much interest in your life and he is hiding the fact that he doesn't know how to handle parenthood. This behaviour also counts as bait in family disputes. Occasions arise when they work behind each other's back, asking you to keep their generosity a secret.

The examples provided fit the conduct of most members in all the groups. Self-evaluation is either unknown or painful in today's society, therefore individuals rely upon members closest to them for judgement. However, the mirrors are set by the personal interests of those holding them.

The strength of the bubble is not equally important for all the members. Those with personal strive move to the periphery, looking for an opportunity to break free and pursue the interest close to their heart. The escape needs careful planning, for others faithful to the core, will do virtually anything to keep them back. Warnings, blackmail and painting a bleak picture of the future as an outsider would surface, representing the wishes of those who remain. These actions test your commitment, patience, and determination for the individual life you set out to achieve. If you yield, you should stay and work for the bubble, until you summon more strength and clearer thoughts for the next available exit. Or just succumb and stay put.

I see these bubbles as star gateways. Each is designed to fit certain energies and support the chosen lifeform. Within, they provide the illusion of security and sustainable livelihood. Nonetheless, they are bubbles, and outside forces, which are designed to override the strength of the glue that holds the structure together, would be able to weaken or completely destroy them. When it happens, the havoc created by the event will push members and sympathisers into the open, to pursue new interests or to fall victims to headstrong organisation bubbles. It is all for the better. Real experiences, life, and thought-changing events only happen outside the comfort zone, when you are on your own, and you think of yourself only.

I know it sounds awfully selfish in the fashionable sense. Nevertheless, it is your life and you need to make it work the way you want. Think about it! If you do not look after yourself, you will never have the capability to look after anybody else and your contribution will not prove useful for the groups to which you happened to belong. You can only be truly appreciated if you love yourself. And since you are a human being, you have flaws and merits. You might become a dictator without appreciating yourself but love the power, and conduct your actions through sustaining the fear you sowed into the minds of members.

The key to the metaphysics of relationships and fulfilling interactions lies in certain understandings.

> ❖ Life is yours to win. It is a learning platform where you gain experiences and invest them into practice.

❖ All human beings are equal. Under the skin, and regardless of the intentionally targeted social, financial and political background, we are of the same organic structure, living on Earth with a shared purpose of evolutionary growth.

❖ Souls choose their families. Human procreation provides a suit for aspiring souls to come and learn the somewhat limited existence on the planet. Families and circumstances are selected to fit prior plans and evolution structures. In a conventional sense, I would say that souls do not have colour.

❖ Since we live in interrelations every soul and its commitment to the planet is important. Responsibility for individual deeds thought and words should be taken and extended to that of other human beings.

- ❖ Roleplays, such as parenting, children, other family members, colleagues and countless more, are there to support the learning procedure. None of us carries the knowledge assigned to us in the conscious but we learn on the road. We excel in some and not much in others. It is vital to understand this thought.

- ❖ Everybody is doing 100% of their capability at every given moment. According to the circumstances sometimes it is more, other times it is less but never below or over the momentary personal best.

- ❖ Emotions are the machinery of life. Without them, the motion of existence stops.

- ❖ Comfort zones are for existing not for living. Answers to questions cannot be found there.

Roles should not replace personal aims. Having a role is not life's achievement only a tool through which new experiences can be taken. Being a child doesn't diminish responsibilities and a parent should not forget individual aims and dreams.

"Material wealth you can inherit, however, true dignity needs to be earned"

AKIA-PATH-FINDER 8

EMOTIONS

The life-giving and saving motion of energies derive from the interrelations of emotions. Emotions are the machinery of life. Without them, organic energies would not survive.

I remember one day sitting in a garden restaurant in Budapest, sipping wheat beer with my students and their colleagues from work, when one started to talk about his relationship, putting emphasis on his abrupt behaviour towards the girlfriend. I knew he was fishing for some professional advice that I am always very happy to give when having fun. I asked him what the trigger of his conduct was. He said he did not know. It just came from nowhere. When I asked him to classify where nowhere was, he motioned to the air around us. I looked at him perplexed. He was an engineer who worked with numbers and facts, even though he was comfortable saying that. Then I told him that nowhere is somewhere, otherwise, it wouldn't exist. And if it doesn't exist, nothing can come from there. Not even emotions. Now, I became the centre of confused glances. But after a short silence, they all started to smile and reassured me that I was right.

If you think about it, we are very comfortable with a certain explanation. We take them on board without giving them a thought. However, everything is logical in life and happens for a reason. Nothing comes from nowhere! Nowhere doesn't exist.

Emotion is the motion of thoughts and thoughts are the mirrors of understanding. It is not very strange really for who you are and what you do, reflect the mental grab of what you know. Knowing is very tricky. We use the word the same way we live; without thinking about its meaning.

Knowing means that you understand something fully, within the interrelations of events. Knowing is experiencing and learning from it. The danger of using this word lies in believing in being accurate. I would not say true as that is another word for the mirror. There is no such thing on Earth we can call truth. Or yes but then we need to take it on board with a pinch of salt. Everybody's truth about the same event is different.

Let me give you an example: I love Mexico. I visited the country on a number of occasions. For years I have been thinking of moving there for people are nice, the food is good, the weather is excellent and the whole Mayan approach is peaceful. However, at the time I mentioned my last trip to people around, they looked at me perplexed, some even with a hint of disgust. When I asked questions, none of them could come up with any kind of experience there. They mentioned drugs, but aren't they everywhere? They did a survey and measured the cocaine substance in the air of Madrid and it topped the chart. Even the US comes long before Mexico in drug consumption! They also say there is a danger that comes from the mentioned problem. Again, isn't it everywhere? Most killings in Spain are drug-related, but the media doesn't connect the two and not announcing the country as dangerous. People are very happy to take their dream holidays on the Costas without giving it another thought.

One of my sisters lives in Canada and she said that she would not go to Mexico because they kill Canadians. Wow, these Mexicans are pretty clever people! How do they know who is Canadian? It is not an ethnic group, anybody could be taken as a citizen of the country. You see, people just follow ideas, the mind manipulation of the media and imagination, supported by their fear of the unknown. Believe me, it is an extraordinary place that I had the privilege of visiting on more than one occasion.

In this story which viewpoint is true? Both of them or you might say none. And since the media gives you plenty of advice on relationship issues, you really need to start thinking and find real values behind the mass consciousness.

My story also serves as an example of emotion altering and mind manipulation. The more you know the less manipulated you are.

I do not get into the details of what it is you need to understand because it is everything. It is the whole existence, your family, friends, how to work, behave, dress, treat yourself and do certain chores. Life is an evolution of the mind and emotions.

SELF LOVE

It is safe to state that love is life for love cannot stop. It has to entail everything and everybody. Loving doesn't mean that you cannot get angry or sad. It means that love doesn't stop just because you are angry. It is always there, running in the background and keeps you on the path. This behaviour is only possible if you love yourself. There are many courses that are teaching you all kinds of methods of loving the self nevertheless, it is very simple really.

You look at yourself as a unique and valuable creation of the universe who is there to add to the constant motion of life in whatever way possible. Here I could say that you love your flaws and merits however, in unconditional love there no flaws and merits. Only an earthling who give their 100% at every given moment.

I am aware of the difficulties this approach would present you, for human beings tend to look at the self through the eyes of others. Therefore it is easier to fall back into the judgemental category rather than rise above it all. The lack of intelligence in others would awake the doubts in your understanding that are sleeping in the back of your mind. Questions such as *what if I wasn't good enough? what if I wasn't beautiful enough? what if I wasn't clever enough?* would rapidly emerge and ruin the concept you built. And ruin your life with it if you are not careful. Take the question time! Grab a pen and paper and write the pros and contras on it. When finished, go through the list once again. The aim is always going forward and not falling back therefore, the focus should be on working the contras. Although you cannot force others to alter their understanding of life but you can gradually turn them towards learning more. And it is a huge achievement. How do you do that?

First of all, you shouldn't project your doubts about your self-value out for others to see. It shows weakness and vulnerability and the sharks follow blood. It is easier to inflict a wound on the already hurt. And by doing it satisfaction of righteousness is built.

Secondly, you have to carry the joy of life with you. Many would find your attitude annoying in the beginning but persistence will achieve gradual admiration, for it takes courage to do it.

"Everything you can touch is lent to you for this life. When you leave, you cannot take anything with you"

AKIA-PATH-FINDER 9

INSECURITY

Insecurity is an illusion. It is the picture created in your mind about the perception of others concerning your qualities. It is the fear of being figured out. The dread of not being perfect. Although perfection is a relative term of understanding, the media is pushing humanity towards owning up to ever more flaws and spending money on trying to correct them, or the medication to surpass the anxiety caused. Earthlings are consciously pushed to their limits by the power struggle of pharmaceutical companies and their agents in modern medicine. It means that publications convey the message of imperfection and the possibilities to remedy it with the help of money. However, this action leads to further uncertainty about the skills to produce more of the *new almighty* and the most lethal catch-22 of earthy existence is formed. The only way out of this trap is through learning.

This concept raises the decisive question: what is it we need to learn? The answer is: we need to understand the self and humanity with it. We need to realise that comprehending life is not an option but an essential ingredient of existence. The one thing we need to conquer on the way is insecurity.

The level of insecurity mirrors the mental and emotional intelligence of the bearer hence, emphasises the lack of information on the mind and the psychological structure of the human race. Without this knowledge, the barrier between the changeable and unchangeable disappears that paves the road towards years of struggle with wasted energies.

Insecurity is one of those fashionable floating feelings that could easily engulf you if not stopped on time. In today's society, we insure the insurance that seemingly protects the house or car we might not even own.

Think about it! If life and your parents treat you well, by the time you become an adult legally, apart from enabling you to buy and consume alcohol at a public place, you collect enough mental and emotional intelligence to take on a paid job. It is the first step towards adulthood, regardless of what you have in your mind and what your parents tell you. They might want you to stick around to fulfil their needs of belonging and achievement. It is especially true with mothers, whose life's purpose stopped at having children and cannot deal with the fact of them leaving the nest. Or they change the course of your life by saying that you should find your dream job first. Well, it is a dangerous path for many reasons.

Who will decide what your dream job is? Although your parents say they know better, they don't. It is an assumption rather than a fact, for everybody's experience is unique, tailored for the individual need of the human being. Unless they are oracles, there is not much chance of seeing your life path and understanding the ways to approach it. They might convince you that want to spare you heartache and struggle, and the word security enters the conversation. And when it appears, it is like a bug in the ear; keeps buzzing until drastically removed by operation. However, the aftermath sensation stays for long. Years later, when you are still searching for the perfect employment, your parents have lost the initial enthusiasm to keep you around. However, while waiting, life passed you by and your CV doesn't have enough entry to be used as a passport to a favoured employment.

With this chain of events, you've arrived at a breaking point in your life. It is time to cut your losses and start anew. Or simply start. Nevertheless, your initial enthusiasm for an independent life is now flattened, your parents are not nearly as supportive as they were at the time of keeping you at home, and since you haven't experienced much, your courage has faded. You see life as an engulfing mystery that eats you up and spits you out. It is time to understand that you have choices. It is also time to find out what these choices are.

❖ You seek professional help, assess your abilities, build up your courage, and make a tangible plan to break away on your own. I need to emphasise that it is essential to find valuable assistance. Without it, you are just spending money and energy.

❖ This is the choice when you are just wasting yourself. Although you look for professional help, however instead of working towards your freedom, you blame life, fate or whatever you prefer to call it, along with your difficult childhood, your parents, your education and the misfortune of being born into your background. This attitude takes you to a *professional* with textbook knowledge who partners with you in the finger-pointing and willingly supports your attitude. The aim of the never-ending string-therapy sessions becomes the *how to bear this cross* rather than easing the burden and make life more joyous.

It is like being buried alive. Due to self-pity, you fall prey to your lack of courage or limited willingness, and instead of changing your life, you start raising your voice in order to gain justification and sympathy for your newly gained victim status. At the end your insecurity might ease, for you will not feel alone anymore however, life will pass you by while getting cosy in your bubble.

❖ The third option is to give in completely, succumb to medication and let yourself be declared mentally dysfunctional.

There are also traditions and religions to talk about. The insecurity we gain from religious beliefs would lead us to become part of the global mass consciousness when we follow ideas without questioning them. We believe that they are a follower of the truth. Yes, but what is truth? And whose truth is truer?

Truth is an illusion, for it is different for everybody. It is the straight result of the intelligence, experience and belief system of the individual or group of people concerned. Bear in mind the fact that we do not actually see what is really there. The eye initially absorbs the rays of light reflected from the object or subject and sends an impulse to the Conscious and the Subconscious at the same time, waiting for their agreement to create a picture consider the Truth by the owner.

We also need to touch upon the subject of spirituality. It is again a belief that spirituality comes with religion and they embrace. I would like to shed some light on the fundamental difference between the two.

Religion glorifies qualities unattainable for you, while spirituality shows you the path to become one with the creator force.

The belief system is changeable by experience, knowledge, openness, and tolerance. I am convinced that creating your own private consciousness would raise the quality of life, and you could look upon Earth as Heaven.

I am certain, many of you find my words harsh, even abrupt from time to time. Nevertheless, I am here to help you and not to agree with you.

Clarity can only come from naked truth. I also want to push you out of your comfort zone to refresh your thoughts and gain the necessary courage to elevate your life to the love affair you deserve.

My final note on insecurity is that it comes from within. Regardless of what others think or say, if you do not believe in your capabilities and values, it will haunt you until you do. Perfection is manmade and relative. There is no human being without flaws and merits.

"Only through the Universe you can reach yourself"

AKIA-PATH-FINDER 10

EMPATHY

In our fast-changing, always challenging and
sometimes overwhelmingly difficult life we learn
to appreciate if someone connects to our
feelings; especially when they are the result of
some sort of suffering. We also tempt to favour
compassionate people.

In my logical and interrelated world, now I've
arrived at a point when further investigation or
explanation is needed if I intend to pursue the
original goal set out in this chapter. The common
understanding of an empath is being sensitive to
the degree of transferring someone's feelings on
the self. My confusion comes from the fact that I
fail to see the value in this behaviour.
Nevertheless, declaring yourself an empath
would gain substantial recognition, even
admiration from people at large. Digging into it
deeper, I realise that these so-called sensitive
earthlings favour suffering over joy, for I yet to
see an empath who is clever enough to find

someone's overwhelming zest for life irresistible and copy the feeling.

Empathy usually needs 2 participants. The one who suffers, and the other one, who takes the feeling on board seemingly without any particular reason. Since similar energies like each other, it becomes obvious that the two of them have alike relations to the subject matter. This understanding derives from social background, upbringing, belief systems and spiritual understanding of life. It means that if a friend complains about her husband cheating on her, I would develop empathy only if I was convinced that it was an unacceptable behaviour within a unity. I might also feel connected if I have already experienced it at one stage and I still carry hurt or dreading it to become reality in my own life. Either way, my reaction says more about my comprehension of existence than being compassionate towards another earthling since their feeling would only remind me of my unsolved issues.

There are people, who would take on a feeling to the extent of developing a particular illness related to the other person. If let's say your digestive system is suffering, and you have a constant stomach ache as the result of some emotional upheaval, the empathic person would create the same illness even if there seem to be no trauma behind the scene in their life. It actually happens because this person has an inclination towards not only the suffering part but the particular thought form that caused it. The digestive system physically suffers as the result of chewing on thoughts that bother us without being able to release them. The reason behind it is fear.

Fear from the future, the past, the present, people around, the family the religion. Let us stay with the example I used earlier. You think that your husband is cheating on you. You will nurture the thought for a while for you are afraid to face the situation, come out and ask him. First of all, you wouldn't think that he was going to tell you the truth. So much for the relationship. However, with this idea, you have already planted doubt, the strongest seed for suffering, for whatever he says you won't believe, and at this point, your partnership is over; unless you change your mind and carry on loving him unconditionally. Well, it is not an easy road but changing is possible.

Taking the first approach on board you would waste time and effort on seeking out others with similar experiences or those who would show empathy. You would reassure yourself that you are not alone with your problem, also you would be able to come out and admit that you are a victim. This way you could all suffer together strengthening the feeling in each other by belonging to the group of *good* people who are taken advantage of by the *bad* ones.

The theory of the sufferers being good comes from modern Christians or I would say from the New Testament where everybody who suffers is called good or saint. We use the term, *yes, she is a saint she suffered enough*, quite loosely in our everyday living without actually giving it a thought. Suffering is a choice. However, it might come from the misconception that life on Earth is suffering and those who suffer go to Heaven, whatever and wherever it is.

Although we are here to learn that we go through experiences and it might take us into the state of momentary suffering, nevertheless, every experience should end with a closure rather than preventing us to get into new tasks of learning and carry on with living and not existing.

There is another type of empathy towards those we consider less fortunate than us because of mental or physical handicaps and other suffering-related events. Spiritually speaking their lives is the result of choices the soul made before coming down to Earth in order to help with learning, experiencing and evolving. Although, these groups need attention, by giving it to them we are actually stating that they are less fortunate. This is also one of life's catch-22.

As a healer and counsellor, I often develop momentary empathy towards my patients to help understand the task ahead of me. However, as the most important part of my work, I would urge and help them to assess the past, take an inventory of it, and look forward to life without the burdens.

I also need to address the meaning of sensitivity. Since every earthling has working senses, we are all sensitive to a certain degree. This degree depends on the emotional and mental intelligence of the human being. Enlightened people are consciously working on these factors to elevate the quality of their living and the lives of those around them. Unfortunately, today's education considers most body functions instinctive, I hope time will come, when walking, talking, seeing, hearing, touching, smelling and other important tasks the body fulfils, will be made conscious by teaching them in schools. Summing empathy up, the realisation should strike, that nobody benefits from it. Only instead of one person now two suffers. Comforting suffering might bring momentary satisfaction but the window on life slowly closes if not opened ajar.

Strangely enough, we do not seem to take on joy or happiness from others. As if we were ashamed of being happy. With this thought, I created a group of HAPPINESS CHAMPIONS where I urge the members to use Empathy in spreading the words of JOY, HEALTH and HAPPINESS.

Well, when you are ready come and knock on my door.

*"The light embraces you unconditionally and
disappears within if you let it"*

AKIA-PATH-FINDER 11

ANXIETY

It comes from a sudden realisation that something is not solved, something is unseen, and something new is entering life.

Anxiety is a blockage in clear thinking, as if existence stopped, due to the cut in the oxygen supply of the brain. However, an important clarification is needed to emphasise that the attack is not the result of the lack of oxygen but the anxiety attack halts the oxygen flow. It is a safety mechanism, much like the security doors in financial institutions, such as banks. When the system senses something unknown or suspicious, it triggers the doors and closes the escape routes. In the case of the brain, it prevents painful, undesired thoughts and feelings from penetrating the comfort zone.

In today's world, anxiety is far more common than it was, let's say 50 years ago. This fact is due to the undisputed reign of social media where individuals and groups are constantly judged for either doing something different or following fashionable views. Regardless of the outcome, one needs to be pretty resilient to withstand the pressure coming from society.

The trap is in the illusion of safety, belonging and togetherness, provided by the never-ceasing posts, chats and group actions pouring out of your telephone, iPad and other internet capturing devices. Just think about it! How much of your valuable time do you spend on second-rate, even third-rate subjects or conversations? This time is taken out of your life. This is time you lose. It never comes back. You grant this time to purposeless thoughts and events while you are afraid of changes, and anxiety sets up camp in your brain. In this process, important decisions would fail you and take you further away from seeing, understanding and experiencing. What is it you need to see, understand and experience? The reality around you. Your place in society.

Your duties, your contribution and
responsibilities.

As we all know, medication is not healing the
illness but concealing the symptoms by sending
you into the pink clouds so you are unable to see
the core of the matter.

Your key sentence should be:

*Living is an elevated and conscious state of
existence!*

The choice is yours. It is your life. In foundation
that is. However, since we live in interrelation,
your choice will affect the lives of those around
you and they will affect the lives of those around
them, and so on. If you consider this point, you
owe it to not only yourself but to humanity at
large to learn, to get better at facing situations
and gather the courage to take the necessary
steps towards solving them.

In case, and I sincerely hope it is, your choice is to rise above fear, you need to look for help. This help should not necessarily be coaching. I would advise on learning about life and emotions. A course where the structure of spending time on Earth would be explained and put into practice. Where thoughts would be organised, monitored and clarified. A course where knowledge is gained and implemented into existence.

I wholeheartedly recommend any of my courses. Check them out on my website.

"Imagination is the memory of the soul"

AKIA-PATH-FINDER 12

DEPRESSION

Depression is one of the commonest yet, the most complex mental disorders, for the state and the root of the illness are unique to every person. Like with everything, modern medicine is only capable of providing information on the symptoms rather than the cause. Let's see what is behind this almost fashionable mental disorder that feeds half of the coaching and therapeutic community.

Its most ordinary cultivation ground is the result of a so-called bad choice. It is not that surprising, for every moment in life is an outcome of a conscious or subconscious selection. A choice is conscious if it sparks a debate in the mind of the owner. However, paying attention to every step in all aspects of life is very difficult indeed. Adding to the initial challenge is the fact that a choice awakens a plan and puts it on a road. From this moment on, this journey needs constant monitoring, unless it runs on autopilot.

The more the choices, the more confusing it becomes to deal with the additional workload and it is inevitable that some of these projects end up in a swamp, in another word, depression. It is very well to abandon projects, for you cannot carry on with everything once started. New ventures seem more exciting than old ones, especially if the latter hit the *getting difficult* state. And excitement you need. Temporary anxiety, to create or perform something new, will bring in all kinds of emotions, allowing the life elixir to flow and build the necessary channel for fire and knowledge.

However, caution should be observed. Unfinished businesses are like hooks, holding you back and tie you to the past, adding a dose of disappointment to the present. Family members step in, friends and acquaintances will justify their judgement and after multiple abandonments, the adjective *looser* begins circulating behind your back at first, and casually at your face later. This commonly human approach leaves a stain on your behaviour, and depending on your mental and emotional intelligence, would push you towards new ventures and the desire to take them to success, or make you withdraw and stop venturing.

Since life is in constant motion, idle stopping is not a good choice, for it could easily end up in a feeling of not belonging, not being good enough, the whole life is against me and I do not want to be hurt. These are the ingredients of depression. On the other hand, constant excitement searching could take you to anxiety. You might not achieve anything you plan but you will have sufficient life elixir to carry on.

As you see, the catch-22 trap is at work again. You need to learn how to balance or harmonise each journey. Earthlings remember the words balance and harmony that is why they are seeking them continuously. However, they misinterpret these expressions. Permanence doesn't exist due to the ever-changing motion in the universe.

There are two keys to tackle depression. The first would be the fact that bad choices do not exist, for one is presenting the 100% of one's capabilities in every moment. It means that one cannot choose differently. It also means that you cannot carry on lamenting your misfortune of bad choices. You took them to learn and add to your knowledge.

The other key is life itself. Many earthlings blame all their sorrow on life. Well, life is a choice although, it might not be obvious without understanding the concept.

In general, coming down to Earth is a choice. Therefore, turning away from earthly life is not an option. Hiding behind dogmas and excuses, spare the self from hurt, disappointment, and sorrow. On the other hand, it is an existence without the wonderful experiences of everyday events.

Living in the physical body, yet putting the everyday maintenance chores on the shoulders of fellow earthlings, is an unfair deed. Furthermore, these beings use the most common blackmailing system, the raising of guilt in the uncertain and undecided minds. They might even say what they do is a sacrifice and that it is done for the benefit of others, sometimes even the whole of mankind. Do not be fooled! It is a selfish act, to serve the ego by seemingly becoming egoless.

I am referring to certain religious groups where collecting donations and begging on the street are part of everyday existence to maintain their idle, unproductive lives. It is easy to say that *I do not agree with capitalism, I do not like the money centred society and so on.* If you don't like it, do something about it. Lifestyles and societies do not spring from the ground by themselves. The seed was sown and the land was cultivated. You are part of it, and as a human being, you share the responsibility with others. It strikes me, how easily earthlings are manipulated and how little they think. Not succumbing to consumerism personally but living on someone, who might not have this convenient choice, doesn't make you a better person, only a parasite. It is true for family connections also.

"The true knowledge is untouchable and changing"

AKIA-PATH-FINDER 13

DECISION MAKING

Medically, the lack of decision-making abilities is not considered an illness however, it could be a firm ground for mental disorders.

It all comes down to learning and understanding that everybody performs 100% of their capabilities at every given moment. It is always the momentary best that shines through with the decision-making. Therefore, the past should be never be looked at as a failure but be assessed and learned from.

Let me elaborate on this idea. Life is in constant motion. It means that you can never go back to a place where you have been before or expect the same consideration you have experienced before. It has nothing to do with better or worse. These are relative comparatives, they only depict momentary feelings, created by the mental and emotional intelligence of the individual.

Comparison is deadly. It could actually ruin your life, since you can only use your experience as the base for the act. And this base is limited. You might borrow a superficial ground, such as being a millionaire, a prince, a famous person, and announce it to be the superlative in your judgement. However, you forget to consider the personal changes you would need to go through to enable yourself of managing the new lifestyle. Your friends would change, your place would change, your work would change and your interest would shift.

Nothing ever is the same. Even your place! You leave in the morning and close the door behind you. When you arrive back, with the thought of coming home, stepping into your comfort zone, you will find different energies there. This change might not be noticeable, for it happens gradually. Until one day, you go through a major influence that triggers your mind and opens some knowledge in the subconscious while away from the comfort zone. Upon arrival, you open the door and look around surprise that you have been living there and found the place very agreeable before.

Change is good. You need to accept the fact of motion in your life and the universe. Therefore, decision making is a daily routine. Bad and good decision do not exist. There are only decisions. Regardless the direction they will always take you forward. Even if the fear-filled emotions tell you otherwise. The U-turns and loopholes are for learning and experiencing. They add to your vision and skills, so you'll be ready for the aim, you are pursuing.

Do not forget, you are the master! They are your emotions and your life. And the master always wins! Open your mind, your life, learn from events and others: allow your emotions to flow. However, you need to maintain control at all times. Not a tight one, only 2%, if you are brave. Losing the driving seat means that you are not going anywhere, so you miss the experience. You have to shine through every cloud and fog.

I am certain you have realised that you notice different things when you are driving and when you are being a passenger. Unless you are so controlling that watch every move the driver makes. Well, it is another experience. The moral of the story is that you need to trust the driver if you decide on the passenger seat.

When you are driving, you have to have total control of the road and the vehicle. There is no time or possibility to notice anything else. However, when you are driven, you can look around, notice events and your thoughts can flow freely. But you are not in control of the road, the direction the journey is taking you, and the machine. From a learning and enjoyment point of view, the best approach is between the two. You always need to have some control over the road. The how much depends on your courage and trust in yourself.

So when you arrive home from a party announcing that: it was great! I got stoned, and I do not remember anything, would pause a valid question. What was so great about it? Wasn't it a waste of time and effort? It is only an experience if you are able to recollect it and use it.

Remember, life is yours to win!

"Life is an elevated, conscious state of existence"

ZSA ZSA TUDOS

TOGETHERNESS

If you want your life to progress, you have to expand your relationship with life. It is like a friendship or a love affair. The interaction is important, for it generates emotions, the fuel that enables you, not only to carry on but to improve. In this book, we talked about different aspects of The Knowledge, the human brain, and the values a soul should chase while living on Earth. Every sentence has a keyword, the one in this is living. As we established earlier, the universe is a matrix. It is logical, for otherwise, it would fall apart. It means that a vast web of interrelated existences creates a pretty neat structure of organic energies. When I say organic energy, it means a living substance. I wouldn't connect intelligence to it because it is one of those expressions that carry a different meaning for everybody. For earthlings, it is given that they are the most intelligent on the planet. However, I beg to differ. Vegetation possesses the laurel for being a perfect link between the micro and the macrocosm, and the most conscious part of the earthly cycle. It is naïve to imagine that vegetables cannot think, hold a conversation or feel. Just because they do not wiggle their tails, they know exactly what goes on around them. If you think about it, everything was a living substance at one point, sprung out of a blend of energies in the cycle of nature. However, earthlings do not appreciate anything with consciousness they cannot fully control. They struggle hard to bring them down to their own level, where higher energies suffocate. This practice is also common amongst their own kind. Today, the great majority of earthlings are floating. They avoid commitments and responsibilities and look for ways to be fed and looked after, rather than building the foundation to stand on. These people are stuck to Air element without understanding Water and Earth. It is an unfortunate situation for without comprehending these two, the path to Fire is concealed. The only way is backwards. However, there is a way.

On the other end of the pole, there are those fully committed to consumerism. They only believe in what they see – which is obviously very limited – build their material wealth, indulge the physical body and go through their chosen experiences in life. This group of earthlings is connected to the Earth element. Sometimes they hit Water and very seldom arrive at the level of Air. Fire avoids this group also.

If I had to, I would definitely vote for the latter. They work, they use their minds and they even exercise their physical body and look after it. They also play with emotions, and one day, they might just wake up with the desire to change! To reach the macrocosmic Fire element from Earth through Water and Air, as the major stations of evolution, is a strong possibility. On the other hand, reaching for the macrocosm without understanding the micro is a definite shift of responsibilities.

Every human relationship is based upon the evolutionary state of the self. In the interrelation, individuals should learn from each other through unconditional trust and love. This type of love is helpful and emotionless; the secret of which is to understand the fact that earthlings perform 100% of their abilities at every given time. It is only expectation that belittles the performance.

To sum up the four basic elements and the evolutionary level, I state the following:

- ❖ EARTH teaches attachments and detachments concerning material. Without understanding both ends, one becomes the slave to money and tangible goods that prevents any kind of evolving. One might reach the six figures in monthly, even daily income, become the wizard of the stock market, would be able to buy material, take the physical body to another level but conscious living would elude these people. The believers of the material world – meaning, what I see is there – are in this category.

❖ WATER opens up emotions, and presents the possibility of understanding and conquering them. Without this kind of knowledge, these people become self-centred and victims of their limited choices. People with strong religious convictions belong here.

❖ AIR is the pathway between the 2 cosms, the Micro and the Macro. It is a floating existence between two planes where the only possible way out is a U-turn. Gurus and Yogis are part of this group.

❖ FIRE comes from the universe. It is Knowledge, Light, and Wisdom. Depending on your state of mind, this element burns or builds. The lack of experience and understanding would result in burns, while Knowledge, based on a solid foundation would prove building. The latter can only be achieved by following, **The 4th Way.** If you wish to know more about the subject, please check out my book with a similar title. It provides you with explanations and exercises built from scratch level.

The summary above shows you that you cannot run without knowing how to walk. Look at a lifetime: a toddler runs before walking. He does it by instinct. And because it is physically easier for him. Nevertheless, he has to learn to walk in order to run consciously. A teenager runs up on stairs skipping 2-3 because he subconsciously believes that he created the universe. He doesn't pay attention to the bone structure and the proper way of doing it. An elderly person would savour each step on the stairs, consciously or maybe only subconsciously understands that everything needs proper foundation and attention.

It means that you have the choice of skipping however, you have to come back to the missed steps if you want to walk with holding your head high and looking down on your achievements without feeling dizzy.

The 4th Way is the only path to a fulfilled life. Living through and understanding the first 3 elements, the FIRE would feel comfortable. I'd like to mention it here that there is a video exercise with the 4 elements meditations on my website ex-files.org that would teach you the basic healing and cleansing ways to keep yourself safe.

Next to the years passed, the other era earthlings obsessed with is the future. However, it usually brings you to shiver for different reasons. The beginning of the future is always unclear, so is the end. This uncertainty causes a lot of difficulties where the time still to come is concerned. The flood of questions would keep you back from entering into the territory. What if

I made the wrong decision? What if I didn't succeed? What if I did succeed? What if I lived, what if I died? Suddenly every plan, wish or desire collapses and builds a wall between the now and then. The mind is switched to pause, while time passes and life goes on. In the meantime, the present is forgotten.

There is a common mistake earthlings do when something interesting or exciting is promised by the future. They dream about it. They want to jump over time to be there as soon as possible, you know, like skipping steps, without realizing that the present – considered to be the real-time life - is passing them by and they miss out on experiences, chances and learning possibilities while eagerly pulling the future nearer. Wishing for the future is just as bad as living in the past. Although time is constantly slowing, it cannot be stopped.

In life, everybody and everything is a mirror that needs to be used for evaluation purposes.

As my experience shows, harmony or balance is widely misunderstood amongst earthlings. Out of the few goals we aim for, this is the most common. We never stop dreaming about it however, deeds usually stay in the background or starts an unrelated journey. We have been fed with fairy tales that put in front of us the struggle we need to go through to reach the "and lived happily ever after" state and it is always the consequence of marriage, if I put it loosely, a couplehood, between 2 differently gendered healthy earthlings, with some sort of wealth behind them to support the harmony they are after. This is a symbolic view of earthly living and should not be taken word for word. The "what is important is hidden" theory is in action here once again. Please, read **The Little Prince** by Saint-Exupery! The wedding of the 2 poles means that the interrelations are learned, emotions understood and mastered, and the 2 cosms are united in 1. With the 4 elements existing in harmony, the earthling is ready for the evolution and the quantum leap. This is the marriage we are after; in reality, however, the meaning is concealed behind dogmas, spiritual and religious views that mirror the actual evolutionary level of their creator.

The "live happily ever after" concept depicts the imaginary state earthlings search for. "I only want to be happy! Is it too much to ask for?" we say while waiting for some kind of a miracle, to provide us with the subject or object of our happiness. We do not realize that the question itself is the only obstacle preventing us from reaching a state of harmony. Primarily the sentence is pointed to the Self, and quite rightly I must admit, for happiness comes from within, whatever our understanding of the word is. Nevertheless, we mislead ourselves by pretending to be aware of this. However, on the picture behind this question, there is always somebody taking up a very prominent place in the outcome. Why do we say that "I want to be happy" when it is conditioned on the presence of another person? There are 2 answers to this question: we either do not care or we do not understand. Neither of these conditions takes us closer to the goal, due to the lack of a basic understanding of earthly living. Do not expect life to provide you with goodies, only because you feel superior and above it. Start a conversation, establish the goal and make a move. Otherwise, life doesn't know what you are after. Remember, it is a love affair.

Earthlings are here to evolve through experience. Basically, there are two kinds of experiences: conscious and random. Although they both further the journey, in this case, I talk about spiritual experience and not money-making skills, as I pointed out earlier. Earthlings who are aware of the path set their goals with an understanding that they are only necessary for drawing the initial direction, rather than an aim to reach.

Random experiences are thrown in by the Universe to help the evolutionary journey.

As everything is interrelated, these events are actually the consequences of the energy movements in one's life. Earthlings who are spiritually aware would be grateful for and learn from both. Others would get angry, depressed, hurt and unhappy about the random experiences, and would hurry to reach the consciously set goal without walking the path towards it.

It does not matter which way I look at the interrelation of energies in human relationships, the Self has to be built in order to understand that you are responsible for not only your deeds, words, and thoughts but for those of every human being because you are also affected by their deeds, words, and thoughts.

It is very easy to get lost on the road to fulfilment. However, one thing is for sure: there is no easy way, and spiritual development is a must. The fear of being different keeps a lot of people away from this search and the misconception concerning the meaning of spirituality and religion only adds to the task load. As a reminder, I put it in front of you again.

Religion is a set of beliefs and practices often centred upon specific supernatural and moral claims about reality.

Becoming part of a religious group only requires acceptance of the mentioned beliefs; while spirituality is an individual and sometimes lonely path to walk, in order to become one with the Creator Force and gain the highest level of existence open to earthlings.

Looking at our world at the moment there are different groups, trying to push, sometimes even force earthlings into an agreement of their theories in life, by limiting their views of the Universe and promising salvation for deeds they consider improper for a human being. Needless to say, the choice is yours. Occasionally one might be forced into joining certain assemblies nevertheless, the real and the only freedom dwells in the mind, regardless of the behaviour pattern of the physical body. Only the freedom of thought is not limited by societies and powers. Do not let them win.

Religious groups and individuals who denounce the exchange of energies between earthlings in any way, are hiding away from the pleasure, sorrow, happiness, sadness and the other feelings encountered through this type of exchange. As practice shows, their auras are pale and the fire is missing from them, together with the element of Earth. One might say that being connected to the Creator Force is all one needs and that knowledge finds a way to flow into the consciousness of the individual.

However, we are here to learn and go through certain events and to understand the Creator – meaning the first knowledge that was able to multiply by division – within. Without this wisdom, one cannot get connected to it, through the dividend created between the two worlds. Now that we have the disastrous Covid-19 amongst us, certain religious leaders and many followers would condemn earthlings of different beliefs as the cause of the pandemic. But why does it enter anyone's mind that God or whatever you want to call it, favours one group over the other? Why do people want to side with such a creator force, who wants worshipping and favours and whatever else the leaders decide, to keep them in his/her heart? The whole universe and everything in it is his/her creation! Why would he/she neglect one over the other? Isn't it a really deceitful naturalistic? I think human beings create their Gods to mirror their limited understanding and behaviour pattern.

Here, I would like to give you a story of a student of mine, who also is a good friend, as all my students. She is having physical coordination problems that nobody can diagnose. We have been working on it together. One day, I sent her to a certain place during Alchemy lesson and she came back with the following:

"Back in time, I had a situation where I chose to care about my emotions instead of standing up for myself. I need to learn to set boundaries and it will make me strong again. Nobody will find a reason why my body is deteriorating because it comes from within so stop wasting time and money going to doctors. The only way to eat the fish is to kill it and cut the head of. If I feel sorry for the fish instead of caring about myself, I will stay hungry."

Life is a delicate catch-22. In the cycle, organic energies co-exist by understanding that they are all important, all have purpose and chores to perform, and feed on each other.

Although not the most intelligent but the most complex of them all is humanity. It is due to the fact that earthlings are not born into the cycle of nature on the planet. They need to lift themselves up by raising emotional intelligence and awareness, to actually fit the requirements. Perhaps, it is the reason why those surviving on slow energies, don't care about this cycle, for they lack the understanding and cannot see its importance. The comprehension of the whole scenario is limited. When a human being runs out of control, we usually compare his actions to those of certain animals by saying, that he is a beast and he behaves like an animal. If you think about it, only human beings are capable of killing missions, cruelties, mental and emotional tortures. That is why conscious learning is vital. I have mentioned the micro and the macrocosm a few times in this book. It is time to add some clarification. Everybody's micro and macrocosm are different. The microcosm is the comfort zone that could be the bedroom or the universe. It is the place one understands – or thinks safe - and the rest will be the macrocosm. During our existence we expand the microcosm by learning and experiencing.

The lives of earthlings are filled with illusions. These are imaginary good and bad to ease their fear. Security is one of them. It doesn't exist. The only secure point in their lives is trust in the self. Everything else is in constant motion, therefore changing.

Life is full of choices! Make the choice and pursue it. However, call upon your intelligence when you are at it. Here is my motto again:

"God, give me the Serenity
To accept the thing I cannot change,
Courage to change the things I can,
And Wisdom always to see the Difference."

I wish you a good life!

THERAPY, COUNSELLING AND COACHING

As we established earlier, mental disorders come from fear, the result of confusion in understanding and relating to life and living conditions. In order to lift yourself up from there, you definitely need a good therapist or coach. Although the dictionary differentiates between them, I think, the importance is not in the title and their work can bring the same result. The emphasis is on the quality, and I don't mean expensive and prominent certificates but the knowledge that lends the understanding of how to remove the client from the comfort zone without damaging their trust. Since every person is different, the professional needs to create individual, step-by-step guidance, and be able to alter it if situations deem fit.

There are very few professionals with this absolutely vital quality. Most of them apply textbook templates, stay within their comfort zone and observe the situation from there. Professionals should be ready to challenge their clients with confidence, showing an elevated moral as an example of a better existence. They should point out the sad end of no-changes, draw an honest picture of the rocky path ahead, and assure the clients of their total support. However, regardless of the professional's capabilities, you the client have to want the change.

Coaching, counselling and mental therapy go hand in hand. They are deep, delicate, honest and trusting alliances between two or more people, aiming for the empowerment of the client. It is a true challenge for clients and coaches equally.

AKIA Philosophy®

AKIA carries the total understanding of the interrelation between the micro - and macrocosm, looks upon everything as an essential part of the whole and upon the whole as an essential part of everything, for all organic and inorganic energies enjoy the same level of importance. This belief makes up the strong foundation of **AKIA** philosophy®.

AKIA is the philosophy of the unseen soul and cosmic knowledge. The philosophy that sets you free.

According to **AKIA Philosophy®** everything and everybody is energy in the sense of physics. These energies are either organic - meaning living - or non-organic - meaning not capable of multiplying or any other form of reproduction. These energies have every feature of the energy known in physics. They have speed, frequency, sound, smell, taste, consistency, colour and polarity. All these energies exist in interrelation that produces the motion of life.

The spirituality of mankind started to vanish as The Knowledge was fading. By ignoring the interrelation of energies earthlings were faced with a mass of new and frustratingly unsolvable questions that made life insecure and doubtful. The mad search for answers was launched.

According to **AKIA** one cannot and need not understand everything. That is the profound understanding of this philosophy.

Through the milestones, **AKIA** proves, that one is the whole and the whole is the one, meaning that everything leads back to one source, the Creator. The Creator - let it be a stone, a cloud or a tree - is the first knowledge that was able to multiply by division. Following this sense, a soul is a knowledge that is able to multiply by division.

AKIA says that one can only understand oneself through the Universe. Also says that everything is always in motion and constantly changing. This interrelation of energies warns us that we are responsible not only for ourselves, but everybody and everything for everybody and everything affects us, our state of mind, our way of thinking, health and behaviour pattern.

AKIA has been created and founded by Zsa Zsa Tudos philosopher, teacher, healer, international clairvoyante and author.

AKIA Philosophy® is the registered trademark of our teachings.

https://zsazsatudos.com

INTUITIVE INTIMACY PREMIUM COURSE

https://ex-files.org/intuitive-intimacy-premium-course/

SENSIBLE DATING PREMIUM COURSE

https://ex-files.org/sensible-dating/

REGAIN YOUR TRUST PREMIUM COURSE

https://ex-files.org/regain-your-trust/

SELF-HEALING WITH THE 4 ELEMENTS

https://ex-files.org/healing-with-elements/

LIVING WITH NATURE AS A LIGHTWORKER PREMIUM COURSE

https://ex-files.org/spiritual-nature/

THE ROYAL ART OF KHEM MEGA COURSE

https://ex-files.org/the-royal-art-of-khem/

SOUL READING

https://ex-files.org/soul-reading/

NEWSLETTER & COMMUNITY

https://ex-files.org/stepin/

www.ingramcontent.com/pod-product-compliance
Lightning Source LLC
Chambersburg PA
CBHW031133090426
42738CB00008B/1066